1

For Geri and Steve

# MUFFIN TOP MANIA!

## 51 Sweet and Savory Muffin Top Recipes

By Shashi Charles of Savory Spin

# Table Of
# CONTENTS

# MUFFIN TOP MANIA!

## 51 Sweet and Savory Muffin Top Recipes

By Shashi Charles of Savory Spin

# Table Of
# CONTENTS

# Table Of
# CONTENTS

# Introduction

This muffin top book happened because muffin tops are my favorite part of a muffin. Maybe they are yours too? Or, maybe you are curious to try them out?

Whatever the reason may be, thank you for picking up this book.

There are many reasons why I love muffin tops. For one, I am not a huge fan of the soggy bottom on some of the muffins I have had. So, instead of tearing off the top and only eating it (like a character in a certain sitcom did), I choose to make just the tops of muffins. Second, to me, muffin tops have such an awesome texture. They are firm and ever so slightly crisp on the outside while being cake-like on the inside. And third, they are so easy to make. You do not need a separate muffin pan or many kitchen gadgets and gizmos. In addition to the ingredients, you will need a bowl, a spoon, measuring utensils, a baking tray of some sort, and parchment paper or a Silpat.

While the muffin tops in this book might look like cookies, they actually tend to fall between a cookie and a cupcake in texture. I am a huge fan of texture and flavor so I tried my best to inject delicious flavor into every one of these muffin top recipes. Some of them are flavored with spices and others by the main mix-ins.

Most of these muffin tops are made with a combination of almond flour and all-purpose flour. The reason I didn't use only all-purpose flour on most of these MTs (muffin tops) is because almond flour adds a hint of nutty sweetness as well as moisture and a delightful texture to the muffin tops that all-purpose flour alone just doesn't.

Most of the 51 recipes in this book have similar main ingredients but the quantity of each of these differs ever so slightly for texture and taste. Most of these MTs can be stored in the fridge for 2 weeks or frozen for 2-3 months. They can be thawed out by placing them at room temperature for 30 minutes to an hour.

Each of these muffin top recipes has been made in a gas oven. Most gas ovens tend to have a more humid environment than electric ovens because of the moisture produced during combustion. And, some gas ovens can also vary in temperature to electric ovens. Though, gas ovens tend to vary in temperature from each other as well.

I have made these muffin top recipes easy to make with ingredients that are easy to get your hands on. And, I have had a blast enjoying all these recipes. My hope is that you get as much joy as I have by making and tasting these recipes. Now, let's start baking...

Love,

Shashi

# Muffin Tops For All!
*(some gluten-free, some dairy-free, one vegan)*

*Chock full of fresh cherries, these MTs, are so easy, tasty, and so portable! A batch of these served as an energizing snack during a summer trip to New York, last year. These Chocolate Cherry Muffin Tops managed to stay fresh and delicious even after being exposed to NYC's heat and TSA's radiation!*

# Chocolate Cherry MTs

Yield: 4 Muffin Tops

## Ingredients:

1 cup all-purpose flour

1/3 cup sugar

1/3 teaspoon salt

1 teaspoon baking powder

1 egg

3 tablespoon olive oil

4 tablespoons almond milk

2 teaspoons vanilla extract

1/2 cup fresh cherries

1/2 cup chocolate chips

## Directions:

1. Preheat the oven to 375 degrees Fahrenheit.

2. Add the dry ingredients (all-purpose flour, sugar, salt, and baking powder) to a medium-sized glass bowl, and mix well.

3. Then add the wet ingredients (the egg, oil, almond milk, and vanilla) into the dry ingredients and mix well.

4. Remove the pit from the cherries, and cut them up into large chunks. Then add the cherry chunks to the batter.

5. Add the chocolate chips into the batter as well and mix well.

6. Add spoonfuls of batter onto a silpat lined baking tray, to make 4 muffin tops, gently shaping them as necessary.

7. Bake at 375 degrees for 18-20 minutes.

8. Remove from the oven, let cool, and enjoy!

*These are some of my favorite muffin tops. Ever so slightly crisp on the outside with a soft, moist center filled with chocolate chips, zucchini, and walnuts. The zucchini ads moisture as well as a nice nutritious spin to these MTs! These are so filling and tasty and are a fantastic portable breakfast or snack!*

# Zucchini Chocolate Chip MTs

Yield: 4 Muffin Tops

## Ingredients:

1/2 cup almond flour
1/2 cup all-purpose flour
1/3 cup Truvia® Blend
  (sugar & stevia blend)
1/3 teaspoon salt
1 teaspoon baking powder
1 egg
1 tablespoon grape seed oil
1 tablespoon almond milk
1/3 cup shredded & drained
  zucchini (approximately
3/4 of a zucchini)
1/3 cup chocolate chips
1 teaspoon vanilla extract
1/3 cup walnuts

## Directions:

1. Preheat the oven to 350 degrees Fahrenheit
2. Wash the zucchini well, then pat dry.
3. Using a vegetable grater, grate the zucchini.
4. Then, drain it slightly using a paper towel. Set the grated zucchini aside.
5. Then add the dry ingredients (almond flour, all-purpose flour, Truvia®, salt, and baking powder) to a medium-sized glass bowl, and mix well.
6. Then add in the wet ingredients (the egg, oil, almond milk, and vanilla and mix well.
7. Add in the zucchini (it should still be a bit moist), the chocolate chips and walnuts and mix well. The dough should be thick.
8. Add spoonfuls of dough onto a silpat lined baking tray, to make 4 muffin tops, gently shaping them as necessary.
9. Bake at 350 degrees for 20 minutes.
10. Remove from the oven, let cool, and enjoy!

# Beet Chocolate Chip MTs

Yield: 4 Muffin Tops

## Ingredients:

1/4 cup almond flour
3/4 cup all-purpose flour
1/3 cup sugar
1/3 teaspoon salt
1 teaspoon baking powder

2 tablespoons grated raw beetroot
1 egg
3 tablespoons olive oil
3 tablespoons almond milk
1 teaspoon vanilla extract
1/2 cup chocolate chips

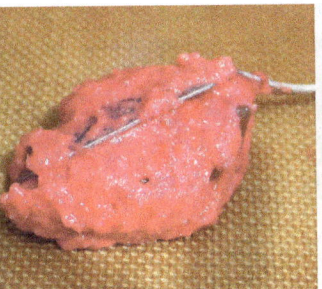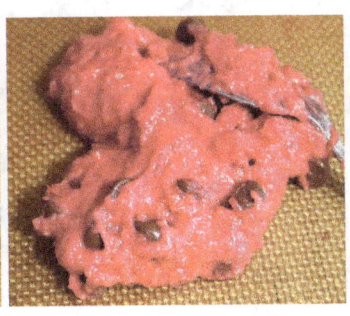

## Directions:

1. Preheat the oven to 375 degrees Fahrenheit.
2. Wash the beetroot well, then pat dry.
3. Using a microplane grater, grate the beetroot to yield 2 tablespoons (approximately about 1/2 a small beetroot). It is important to use a microplane grater and not a vegetable grater as the microplane grater will grate the beetroot into smaller shreds than a vegetable grater would. This would help the beetroot evenly color the MTs.
4. Then add the dry ingredients (almond flour, all-purpose flour, sugar, salt, and baking powder) to a medium-sized glass bowl, and mix well.
5. Then add in the wet ingredients (the grated beetroot, egg, oil, almond milk, and vanilla and mix well.
6. Add in the chocolate chips and fold them into the batter.
7. Add spoonfuls of dough onto a silpat lined baking tray, to make 4 muffin tops. If you want to make them into heart-shaped muffin tops, add the spoonfuls at an angle to each other. Using the back of the spoon, gently nudge the batter into a heart shape.
8. To ensure the batter bakes into a heart-shape, use strips of aluminum foil, shaped into a v, to place into the heart indent at the top of these muffin tops (as seen in the far right diagram).
9. Bake at 375 degrees for 18-20 minutes.
10. Remove from the oven, let cool, and enjoy!

*Avocado takes the place of oil or butter in these muffin tops, resulting in a delightfully light crumb thats ever so slightly crisp on the outside.*

# Avocado Lime Crumb MTs

Yield: 4 Muffin Tops

## Ingredients:

1/2 cup almond flour

1/2 cup all-purpose flour

1/3 cup Truvia® blend
 (sugar & stevia blend)

1/3 teaspoon salt

1 teaspoon baking powder

1 egg

1 avocado

1 tablespoon lime juice

1 lime (zest of 1 lime)

### CRUMB TOPPING

2 tablespoons all-purpose flour

2 tablespoons sugar

1 tablespoon butter (cold)

zest of 1/2 a lime

## Directions:

1. Preheat the oven to 375 degrees Fahrenheit
2. Add the dry ingredients (almond flour, all-purpose flour, Truvia®, salt, and baking powder) to a medium-sized glass bowl, and mix well.
3. Cut open the avocado, spoon out the avocado flesh, add it to a bowl and mash it well.
4. Then add it, along with the wet ingredients (the egg, avocado, lime juice and lime zest) and mix well.
5. Add spoonfuls of batter onto a silpat lined baking tray, to make 4 muffin tops.
6. Make the Crumb topping by mixing together the AP flour, sugar, cold butter, and lime zest, with your hands. Squeeze the butter into the other ingredients, so chunks or crumbs form.
7. Then, sprinkle the crumb topping onto each of the 4 muffin tops. Very gently press down on the crumbs so they stick to the muffin tops, gently shaping them as necessary.
8. Bake at 375 degrees for 20-22 minutes.
9. Remove from the oven, let cool, and enjoy!

# Blackberry MTs

Yield: 4 Muffin Tops

## Ingredients:

1/2 cup almond flour

1/2 cup all-purpose flour

1/4 cup sugar

1/3 teaspoon salt

1 teaspoon baking powder

1/2 teaspoon cinnamon

1 egg

3 tablespoon olive oil

2 tablespoons almond milk

2 teaspoons vanilla extract

1/2 cup fresh blackberries
  (1/4 cup crushed and
  1/4 cup cut in half)

## Directions:

1. Preheat the oven to 375 degrees Fahrenheit.

2. Add the dry ingredients (almond flour, all-purpose flour, sugar, salt, and baking powder) to a medium-sized bowl, and mix well.

3. Then add in the wet ingredients (the egg, oil, almond milk, and vanilla and mix well.

7. Wash the blackberries and pat dry. Then, take 1/4 cup of blackberries and chop them up finely, and add them to the muffin top batter and mix well.

6. Cut the remaining 1/4 cup of blackberries into large chunks and add them to the batter and gently fold them in. The aim is to have big chunks of blackberries to bite into while having that tasty blackberry flavor through out each muffin top.

8. Add spoonfuls of batter onto a silpat lined baking tray, to make 4 muffin tops, gently shaping them as necessary.

9. Bake at 375 degrees for 20-25 minutes.

10. Remove from the oven, let cool, and enjoy!

# Chocolate Pretzel MTs

Yield: 4 Muffin Tops

## Ingredients:

1/2 cup almond flour

1/2 cup all-purpose flour

1/4 cup sugar

1/3 teaspoon salt

1 teaspoon baking powder

1/2 teaspoon cinnamon

1 egg

3 tablespoon olive oil

2 tablespoons almond milk

1 teaspoon vanilla extract

1/2 cup chocolate chips

1/2 cup mini pretzels
  (broken up)

## Directions:

1. Preheat the oven to 375 degrees Fahrenheit.

2. Add the dry ingredients (almond flour, all-purpose flour, sugar, salt, cinnamon, and baking powder) to a medium-sized glass bowl, and mix well.

3. Then add in the wet ingredients (the egg, oil, almond milk, and vanilla and mix well.

4. Add in the chocolate chips.

5. Break up the mini pretzel into smaller pieces, and add them to the bowl as well.

6. Add spoonfuls of batter onto a silpat lined baking tray, to make 4 muffin tops, gently shaping them as necessary.

7. Bake at 375 degrees for 18-20 minutes.

8. Remove from the oven, let cool, and enjoy!

# PB&J MTs

Yield: 4 Muffin Tops

## Ingredients:

1/2 cup almond flour

1/2 cup all-purpose flour

1/4 cup sugar

1/3 teaspoon salt

1 teaspoon baking powder

1/2 teaspoon cinnamon

1 egg

3 tablespoon olive oil

2 tablespoons almond milk

1 teaspoon vanilla extract

3 tablespoons jelly

3 tablespoons peanut butter

## Directions:

1. Preheat the oven to 375 degrees Fahrenheit.
2. Add the dry ingredients (almond flour, all-purpose flour, sugar, salt, cinnamon, and baking powder) to a medium-sized bowl, and mix well.
3. Then add in the wet ingredients (the egg, oil, almond milk, and vanilla and mix well.
4. Add in 2 tablespoons of the jelly mixture, reserving 1 tablespoon to drizzle through the batter, and mix the 2 tablespoons in well.
5. Add in 2 tablespoons of the peanut butter, reserving 1 tablespoon to drizzle through the batter, and mix the 2 tablespoons in well.
6. Then, gently drizzle the remaining jelly and peanut butter so there are "globs" of them through the batter.
7. Add spoonfuls of batter onto a silpat lined baking tray, to make 4 muffin tops, gently shaping them as necessary.
8. Bake at 375 degrees for 20-22 minutes.
9. Remove from the oven, let cool, and enjoy ~ with more peanut butter and jelly!

# Pistachio Rose MTs

Yield: 4 Muffin Tops

## Ingredients:

1/2 cup pistachios
  (to make pistachio flour)
1/2 cup all-purpose flour
1/3 cup sugar
1/3 teaspoon salt
1 teaspoon baking powder
1 egg
2 tablespoon olive oil
1 tablespoons almond milk
1 teaspoon rose water
1/2 a lemon (zest only)
OPTIONAL: dried rose petals
OPTIONAL: pistachio pieces
DRIZZLE
1/4 cup icing sugar
1 teaspoon lemon juice
1 teaspoon rose water

## Directions:

1. Preheat the oven to 375 degrees Fahrenheit.
2. Add the pistachios to a blender (preferably one that grinds nuts) and pulse until the pistachios are ground into a flour-like consistency. However, if you can get your hands on some store-bought pistachio flour, use that instead.
3. Add the dry ingredients (pistachio flour, all-purpose flour, sugar, salt, and baking powder) to a medium-sized bowl, and mix well.
4. Then add in the wet ingredients (the egg, oil, almond milk, rose water, and lemon zest and mix well.
5. Add spoonfuls of batter onto a silpat lined baking tray, to make 4 muffin tops, gently shaping them as necessary.
6. Bake at 375 degrees for 20-22 minutes.
7. Remove from the oven, let cool.
8. Make the drizzle by mixing the icing sugar with lemon juice and rose water, and drizzle on top of each MT. Top with crushed pistachios and dried rose petals and enjoy!

*These Spiced Crumb Muffin Tops are such an indulgent treat. Aromatic and delicious, they pair so well with a cup of coffee or tea. However, I must warn you, while most of the Muffin Tops on here are portable, these guys tend to be a bit messy as that crumb topping has a tendency to get on everything.*

# Spiced Crumb MTs

Yield: 4 Muffin Tops

## Ingredients:

1/2 cup almond flour

1/2 cup all-purpose flour

1/3 cup sugar

1/3 teaspoon salt

1 teaspoon baking powder

1/4 teaspoon cinnamon

1/8 teaspoon cardamom

1/8 teaspoon ginger

1/8 teaspoon cloves

1 egg

3 tablespoons butter (melted)

1 tablespoons almond milk

1 teaspoon vanilla extract

1 tablespoon sour cream

### CRUMB TOPPING

1/2 cup all-purpose flour

3 tablespoons brown sugar

2 tablespoons sugar

1/2 teaspoon cinnamon

1/8 teaspoon salt

3 tablespoons cold butter

## Directions:

1. Preheat the oven to 375 degrees Fahrenheit.

2. Add the dry ingredients (almond flour, all-purpose flour, sugar, salt, baking powder, cinnamon, cardamom, ginger, and cloves) to a medium-sized bowl, and mix well.

3. Then add in the wet ingredients (the egg, melted butter, {BTW, the butter can be melted by placing in a microwave-safe dish and microwaving on high for 20 seconds or so} almond milk, sour cream, and vanilla and mix well and set aside in the fridge, while making the crumb topping.

4. Make the crumb topping by adding the flour, brown sugar, sugar, cinnamon, salt, and cold butter to a bowl and mixing with them together with your hands. Gather the mixture together while mixing to form into crumb chunks.

5. Then, add spoonfuls of batter onto a silpat lined baking tray, to make 4 muffin tops, gently shaping them as necessary.

6. Add the crumb topping on top of each muffin top, very gently pushing the crumb topping into each muffin top.

7. Bake at 375 degrees for 20-25 minutes.

8. Remove from the oven, let cool, and enjoy!

# Blueberry Flax MTs

Yield: 4 Muffin Tops

## Ingredients:

1/2 cup ground flax

1/2 cup all-purpose flour

1/3 cup sugar

1/3 teaspoon salt

1 teaspoon baking powder

1 teaspoon cinnamon

1 egg

2 tablespoons almond milk

2 tablespoon olive oil

2 teaspoons vanilla extract

3/4 cup fresh blueberries

## Directions:

1. Preheat the oven to 375 degrees Fahrenheit.

2. Add the dry ingredients (ground flax, all-purpose flour, sugar, salt, cinnamon, and baking powder) to a medium-sized bowl, and mix well.

3. Then add in the wet ingredients (the egg, oil, almond milk, and vanilla and mix well.

4. Wash the fresh blueberries, pat them dry and then add them into the batter and mix well. The dough should be thick.

5. Then, add spoonfuls of batter onto a silpat lined baking tray, to make 4 muffin tops, gently shaping them as necessary.

6. Bake at 375 degrees for 20-22 minutes.

7. Remove from the oven, let cool, and enjoy!

# Banana Walnut MTs

Yield: 4 Muffin Tops

## Ingredients:

1/2 cup almond flour

1/2 cup all-purpose flour

1/3 cup sugar

1/3 teaspoon salt

1 teaspoon baking powder

1 egg

1 banana

2 tablespoons melted butter

1 tablespoons almond milk

1 teaspoon vanilla extract

3/4 cup walnuts

## Directions:

1. Preheat the oven to 375 degrees Fahrenheit.

2. Add the dry ingredients (almond flour, all-purpose flour, sugar, salt, and baking powder) to a medium-sized bowl, and mix well.

3. Melt the butter by placing it in another microwave-safe dish and microwaving on high for 20 seconds.

4. Then add in the wet ingredients (the egg, melted butter almond milk, and vanilla and mix well.

5. Peel the banana and add it to the bowl the butter was melted in, and mash it. Then add the mashed banana to the batter.

6. Add the walnuts to the batter too and mix the walnuts and banana into the batter.

7. Add spoonfuls of batter onto a silpat lined baking tray, to make 4 muffin tops, gently shaping them as necessary.

8. Bake at 375 degrees for 20-25 minutes.

9. Remove from the oven, let cool, and enjoy!

# Apple Cinnamon MTs

Yield: 4 Muffin Tops

## Ingredients:

1 cup oat flour

1/3 cup brown sugar

1/3 teaspoon salt

1 teaspoon baking powder

1/4 teaspoon baking soda

2 teaspoons cinnamon

1/4 teaspoon cardamom

1/4 teaspoon nutmeg

1/4 teaspoon cloves

1 egg

2 tablespoons almond milk

2 tablespoon olive oil

2 teaspoons vanilla extract

1/3 cup chopped up apples
(approximately 1/2 an apple)

## Directions:

1. Preheat the oven to 375 degrees Fahrenheit.
2. Add the dry ingredients (oat flour, sugar, salt, baking powder, baking soda, cinnamon, cardamom, nutmeg, and cloves) to a medium-sized bowl, and mix well.
3. Then add in the wet ingredients (the egg, oil, almond milk, and vanilla and mix well.
4. Chop up the apple into very small pieces and add it to the batter, and mix well.
5. Let the batter sit for 5 minutes at least so the oats absorb Some of the liquid and batter thickens up some. The batter can be left on the kitchen counter or if the kitchen is too warm, then place it in the fridge.
6. Add spoonfuls of batter onto a silpat lined baking tray, to make 4 muffin tops, gently shaping them as necessary.
7. Bake at 375 degrees for 20-22 minutes.
8. Remove from the oven, let cool, and enjoy!

TIP: *If you have rolled oats on hand, you can use it to make oat flour. Simply add about a cup and a half of rolled oats to a high-speed blender and blend the rolled oats on hight for about 10 seconds or until the oats are ground up into a flour-like consistency.*

# Mung Bean Brown Sugar MTs

Yield: 4 Muffin Tops

## Ingredients:

1/2 cup almond flour

1/2 cup all-purpose flour

1/3 cup brown sugar

1/3 teaspoon salt

1 teaspoon baking powder

1/2 teaspoon ground ginger

1 egg

2 tablespoons olive oil

2 tablespoons almond milk

1 teaspoon vanilla extract

1/2 cup cooked moong/mung beans

## Directions:

1. Preheat the oven to 375 degrees Fahrenheit.
2. First off, let's prepare the mung beans. Add the dry mung beans to a pan filled with water. Run your hands through them to loosen any debris. Then pour the water out. Repeat this until the water runs clean. Then, fill the pan with water so the mung beans are submerged and place it over a stove top set to medium heat. Let mung beans come to a boil and then simmer for about 30 minutes. Drain the mung beans and set aside to use in this recipe.
3. Then add the dry ingredients (almond flour, all-purpose flour, sugar, salt, ginger, and baking powder) to a medium-sized bowl, and mix well.
4. Then add in the wet ingredients (the egg, oil, almond milk, and vanilla and mix well.
5. Add in the cooked mung beans and mix well.
6. Add spoonfuls of batter onto a silpat lined baking tray, to make 4 muffin tops, gently shaping them as necessary.
7. Bake at 375 degrees for 20-22 minutes.
8. Remove from the oven, let cool, and enjoy!

# AB&J MTs

Yield: 4 Muffin Tops

## Ingredients:

4 tablespoons jelly (your favorite brand-frozen overnight)
1/2 cup almond flour
1/2 cup all-purpose flour
1/3 cup Truvia® blend
(sugar & stevia blend)

1/3 teaspoon salt
1 teaspoon baking powder
1 egg
2 tablespoons grape seed oil
2 tablespoons almond milk
2 tablespoons almond butter
1/2 teaspoon almond extract

## Directions:

1. First, spoon 4 (separate) tablespoons of jelly onto a cling wrap-lined or parchment-lined container and form the spoonfuls into 4 discs. Freeze these jelly discs overnight.

2. When ready to make these MTs, preheat the oven to 375 degrees Fahrenheit.

3. Add the dry ingredients (almond flour, all-purpose flour, Truvia®, salt, and baking powder) to a medium-sized bowl, and mix well.

4. Then add in the wet ingredients (the egg, oil, almond milk, almond butter, and almond extract) and mix well.

5. Add a spoonful of batter onto a silpat lined baking tray, to make the base of a muffin top. Repeat this step 3 more times so there are a total of 4 bases of muffin tops.

6. Remove the frozen jelly discs from the freezer and place a frozen jelly disc (the jelly might not be quite fully frozen, but add it anyway) on top of the bases of the MTs.

7. Divide spoonfuls of the remaining batter between the four MTs, covering up the jelly discs as much as possible (as seen in the picture above).

8. Bake at 375 degrees for 18-20 minutes.

9. Remove from the oven, let cool, and enjoy with more almond butter and jelly, if so d desired.

# Carrot Cake MTs

Yield: 4 Muffin Tops

## Ingredients:

1 & 1/2 cup all-purpose flour
1/3 cup sugar
1/3 teaspoon salt
1 teaspoon baking powder
1/4 teaspoon cardamom
1/4 teaspoon cloves
1/4 teaspoon nutmeg
1/4 teaspoon ground ginger
1/2 teaspoon cinnamon
2 eggs
3 tablespoons olive oil
3 tablespoons almond milk
1 teaspoon vanilla extract
1/2 cup grated carrot (about 1/2 a large carrot)
1/4 cup raisins
1/4 cup pecans

**GLAZE**
3-4 teaspoons white vinegar
1/2 cup confectioners sugar

## Directions:

1. Preheat the oven to 375 degrees Fahrenheit.
2. Rinse the carrots well, then pat dry, before grating them using a vegetable grater, and set aside.
3. Then add the dry ingredients (all-purpose flour, sugar, salt, baking powder, cardamom, cloves, nutmeg, ginger, and cinnamon) to a medium-sized bowl, and mix well.
4. Then add in the wet ingredients (the egg, oil, almond milk, and vanilla and mix well.
5. Add in the grated carrot, raisins, and pecans and mix well. The dough will be thick.
6. Add spoonfuls of batter onto a silpat lined baking tray, to make 4 muffin tops, gently shaping them as necessary.
7. Bake at 375 degrees for 18-20 minutes.
8. Remove from the oven and let cool.
9. Then make the glaze by mixing together the white vinegar and confectioners sugar until a thick paste is formed. Drizzle glaze over the muffin tops and enjoy!

# Cookies and Cream MTs

Yield: 4 Muffin Tops

## Ingredients:

1/2 cup all-purpose flour

1/2 cup almond flour

1/3 cup sugar

1/3 teaspoon salt

1 teaspoon cinnamon

1 teaspoon baking powder

2 tablespoons olive oil

2 tablespoons almond milk

1 egg

1 teaspoon vanilla extract

6 oreos roughly chopped up

## Directions:

1. Preheat the oven to 375 degrees Fahrenheit.

2. Add the dry ingredients (almond flour, all-purpose flour, sugar, salt, cinnamon, and baking powder) to a medium-sized bowl, and mix well.

3. Then add in the wet ingredients (the egg, oil, almond milk, and vanilla and mix well.

4. Break or chop up the Oreos into teeny tiny pieces and add these to the batter and mix well. The dough should be thick.

5. Add spoonfuls of batter onto a silpat lined baking tray, to make 4 muffin tops, gently shaping them as necessary.

6. Bake at 350 degrees for 20-25 minutes.

7. Remove from the oven, let cool, and enjoy!

# Cinnamon Oatmeal Yogurt MTs

Yield: 4 Muffin Tops

## Ingredients:

1 cup ground oats / oat flour

1/3 cup Truvia® blend
 (stevia & sugar)

1/3 teaspoon salt

1 teaspoon baking powder

1 teaspoon cinnamon

1 egg

1/4 cup Greek yogurt

2 tablespoons almond milk

1 teaspoon vanilla extract

## Directions:

1. Preheat the oven to 375 degrees Fahrenheit.

2. Add the dry ingredients (oat flour, Truvia®, salt, cinnamon, and baking powder) to a medium-sized bowl, and mix well.

3. Then add in the wet ingredients (the egg, Greek yogurt, almond milk, and vanilla and mix well.

7. Let the batter sit for 15-20 minutes in the fridge. The batter should thicken up as the oats absorb the liquid.

8. Add spoonfuls of batter onto a silpat lined baking tray, to make 4 muffin tops, gently shaping them as necessary. To decorate (if so desired) sprinkle a few intact pieces of oats over the tops of the MTs.

9. Bake at 375 degrees for 18-20 minutes.

10. Remove from the oven, let cool, and enjoy!

*TIP: If you have rolled oats on hand, you can use it to make oat flour. Simply add about a cup and a half of rolled oats to a high-speed blender and blend the rolled oats on hight for about 10 seconds or until the oats are ground up into a flour-like consistency.*

# Brown Sugar Cinnamon Raisin MTs

Yield: 4 Muffin Tops

## Ingredients:

1/2 cup almond flour

1/2 cup all-purpose flour

1/3 cup brown sugar

1/3 teaspoon salt

1 teaspoon baking powder

1 egg

2 tablespoons butter (melted)

1 tablespoon almond milk

1 teaspoon vanilla extract

1/3 cup raisins

### CINNAMON SUGAR DUST

1/4 cup brown sugar

1 teaspoon cinnamon

## Directions:

1. Preheat the oven to 375 degrees Fahrenheit.

2. Add the dry ingredients (almond flour, AP flour, brown sugar, salt, and baking powder) to a medium-sized bowl, and mix well.

3. Then add in the wet ingredients (the egg, melted butter {BTW, the butter can be melted by placing in a microwave-safe dish and microwaving on high for 20 seconds or so}, almond milk, and vanilla and mix well.

4. Add in the raisins and mix until incorporated into the batter.

5. Add spoonfuls of batter onto a silpat lined baking tray, to make 4 muffin tops, gently shaping them as necessary.

6. Bake at 3575 degrees for 20-22 minutes.

7. While the MTs are baking, make the "dust" by mixing together the brown sugar and cinnamon in a small bowl.

8. Remove the MTs from the oven, when done.

9. While warm, dust with the cinnamon and brown sugar "dust," let cool, and enjoy!

# Orange Cranberry MTs

Yield: 4 Muffin Tops

## Ingredients:

1/2 cup almond flour

1/2 cup all-purpose flour

1/3 cup sugar

1/3 teaspoon salt

1 teaspoon baking powder

1 egg

2 tablespoons olive oil

2 tablespoons orange juice

1/2 tsp orange zest

1/4 cup dried cranberries

## Directions:

1. Preheat the oven to 375 degrees Fahrenheit.
2. Add the dry ingredients (almond flour, all-purpose flour, sugar, salt, and baking powder) to a medium-sized bowl, and mix well.
3. Then add in the wet ingredients (the egg, oil, and orange juice, and mix well.
4. Add in the orange zest (when zesting/grating the orange, try not to grate in the white part that is just under the orange skin) as well as the dried cranberries to the batter and mix well.
5. Add spoonfuls of batter onto a silpat lined baking tray, to make 4 muffin tops, gently shaping them as necessary.
6. Bake at 375 degrees for 20-22 minutes.
7. Remove from the oven, let cool, and enjoy!

# Cereal MTs

Yield: 4 Muffin Tops

## Ingredients:

3 cups Cheerios™
  (1 cup ground up Cheerios™)
1/2 cup monk fruit sweetener
1/3 teaspoon salt
1 teaspoon baking soda
2 teaspoons cinnamon
2 eggs
4 tablespoons almond milk
2 tablespoon olive oil
1 teaspoons vanilla extract
1/4 cup Cheerios™ (intact)

## Directions:

1. Preheat the oven to 375 degrees Fahrenheit.
2. Add the Cheerios™ to a blender and pulse until the Cheerios™ resemble a flour-like consistency. This Cheerio™ flour is the "flour" for these MTs.
3. Then, add the dry ingredients (Cheerio™ flour, monk fruit sweetener, salt, cinnamon, and baking soda) to a medium-sized bowl, and mix well.
4. Then add in the wet ingredients (the eggs, oil, almond milk, and vanilla extract, and mix well.
5. Add the intact Cheerios™ (save just a few to use on top as decoration if desired) to the batter and mix well.
6. Add spoonfuls of batter onto a silpat lined baking tray, to make 4 muffin tops, gently shaping them as necessary.
7. Place the intact Cheerios™ saved onto the tops of these MTs.
8. Bake at 375 degrees for 30-35 minutes.
9. Remove from the oven, let cool, and enjoy!

# Nutella Stuffed MTs

Yield: 4 Muffin Tops

## Ingredients:

1/2 cup almond flour
1/2 cup all-purpose flour
1/3 cup sugar
1/3 teaspoon salt
1 teaspoon baking powder

1 egg
3 tablespoons olive oil
2 tablespoons almond milk
1 teaspoon vanilla extract
5 tablespoons Nutella®

## Directions:

1. First, spoon 4 (separate) tablespoons of Nutella® onto a parchment-lined tray/container and form the spoonfuls into 4 discs. Freeze these Nutella® discs overnight.
2. When ready to make these MTs, preheat the oven to 375 degrees Fahrenheit.
3. Add the dry ingredients (almond flour, all-purpose flour, sugar, salt, and baking powder) to a medium-sized bowl, and mix well.
4. Then add in the wet ingredients (the egg, oil, almond milk, and vanilla extract) and mix well.
5. Add in 1 tablespoon of Nutella® into the batter and gently ripple it through the batter so it makes streaks.
6. Add a spoonful of batter onto a silpat lined baking tray, to make the base of a muffin top. Repeat this step 3 more times so there are a total of 4 bases of muffin tops.
7. Remove the frozen Nutella® discs from the freezer and place a frozen Nutella® disc on top of the bases of the MTs.
8. Divide spoonfuls of the remaining batter between the four MTs, covering up the Nutella® discs as much as possible (as seen in the picture above).
9. Bake at 375 degrees for 20-25 minutes.
10. Remove from the oven, let cool, and enjoy!

# Iced Orange MTs

Yield: 4 Muffin Tops

## Ingredients:

1/2 cup almond flour

1/2 cup all-purpose flour

1/3 cup Truvia® blend
  (sugar and Stevia blend)

1/3 teaspoon salt

1 teaspoon baking powder

1 egg

2 tablespoons grape seed oil

1 tablespoon orange juice

2 teaspoons orange zest

**ICING**

1/4 cup powdered sugar

1-2 teaspoons orange juice

extra orange zest to sprinkle on

## Directions:

1. Preheat the oven to 375 degrees Fahrenheit.
2. Add the dry ingredients (almond flour, all-purpose flour, Truvia®, salt, and baking powder) to a medium-sized bowl, and mix well.
3. Then add in the wet ingredients (the egg, oil, and orange juice, and mix well.
4. Add in the orange zest (when zesting/grating the orange, try not to grate in the white part that is just under the orange skin) as well as the dried cranberries to the batter and mix well.
5. Add spoonfuls of batter onto a silpat lined baking tray, to make 4 muffin tops, gently shaping them as necessary.
6. Bake at 375 degrees for 20-22 minutes.
7. Remove from the oven and let cool.
8. When cool, make the icing by mixing together the powdered sugar and orange juice. Drizzle the orange icing over the MTs, sprinkle with extra orange zest, and enjoy!

# Morning Glory MTs

Yield: 4 Muffin Tops

## Ingredients:

1/2 cup almond flour
1/2 cup all-purpose flour
1/3 cup Truvia® blend
1/3 teaspoon salt
1 teaspoon baking powder
1/2 teaspoon cinnamon
1/4 teaspoon cardamom
1/4 teaspoon ginger
1 egg
2 tablespoons olive oil
2 tablespoons almond milk
1/3 cup shredded carrots
1/3 cup walnuts
1/3 cup raisins
1 teaspoon vanilla extract
1/4 teaspoon almond extract
1 teaspoon orange zest
1 tablespoon chia seeds
1 tablespoon flax seeds
1 tablespoon coconut flakes

## Directions:

1. Preheat the oven to 375 degrees Fahrenheit.
2. Rinse the carrot, pat dry and grate it using a vegetable grater.
3. Add the dry ingredients (almond flour, all-purpose flour, Truvia®, salt, baking powder, cinnamon, cardamom, and ginger) to a medium-sized bowl, and mix well.
4. Then add in the wet ingredients (the egg, oil, vanilla extract, almond extract, and almond milk), and mix well.
5. Add in the shredded carrots, walnut pieces, raisins, orange zest, chia seeds, flax seeds, and coconut flakes to the batter and fold them in.
6. Add spoonfuls of batter onto a silpat lined baking tray, to make 4 muffin tops, gently shaping them as necessary.
7. Bake at 375 degrees for 20-25 minutes.
8. Remove from the oven, let cool, and enjoy!

*I make these ones when I have a hankering for some chocolate. Then, I top these with some of my 3-ingredient chocolate mousse (which can be found on my blog https://savoryspin.com/3-ingredient-chocolate-mousse ) and I am in heaven! These muffin tops can also be used to make a trifle, along with that 3-ingredient chocolate mousse and some berries (as pictured on the cover).*

# Chocolate MTs

Yield: 4 Muffin Tops

## Ingredients:

1/2 cup almond flour
1/4 cup all-purpose flour
1/4 cup Hershey's® dark cocoa powder
1/3 cup sugar
1/3 teaspoon salt
1 teaspoon baking powder
1 egg
2 tablespoons olive oil
2 tablespoons almond milk
1 teaspoon vanilla extract

## Directions:

1. Preheat the oven to 375 degrees Fahrenheit.
2. Add the dry ingredients (almond flour, AP flour, Hershey's® cocoa, sugar, salt, and baking powder) to a medium-sized bowl, and mix well.
3. Then add in the wet ingredients (the egg, oil, almond milk, and vanilla and mix well.
4. Add spoonfuls of batter onto a silpat lined baking tray, to make 4 muffin tops, gently shaping them as necessary.
5. Bake at 375 degrees for 18-20 minutes.
6. Remove from the oven, let cool, and enjoy!

# Pumpkin Spice MTs

Yield: 4 Muffin Tops

## Ingredients:

1/2 cup almond flour

1/2 cup all-purpose flour

1/3 cup Sugar + 1 tablespoon sugar to sprinkle on top

1/3 teaspoon salt

1 teaspoon baking powder

1 teaspoon pumpkin pie spice

1 egg

1/4 cup pumpkin puree

2 tablespoons almond milk

1 teaspoon vanilla extract

1/3 cup walnuts

## Directions:

1. Preheat the oven to 375 degrees Fahrenheit.
2. Add the dry ingredients (almond flour, all-purpose flour, 1/3 cup sugar, salt, pumpkin pie spice, and baking powder) to a medium-sized bowl, and mix well.
3. Then add in the wet ingredients (the egg, pumpkin puree, almond milk, and vanilla and mix well.
4. Add in the walnuts and mix well. The dough should be thick.
5. Add spoonfuls of batter onto a silpat lined baking tray, to make 4 muffin tops, gently shaping them as necessary.
6. Sprinkle the tops with the remaining 1 tablespoon of sugar before baking.
7. Then, bake at 375 degrees for 20-22 minutes.
8. Remove from the oven, let cool, and enjoy!

# Cinnamon Date Walnut MTs

Yield: 4 Muffin Tops

## Ingredients:

1/2 cup almond flour

1/2 cup all-purpose flour (AP flour)

1/3 cup sugar

1/3 teaspoon salt

1 teaspoon baking powder

1 teaspoon cinnamon

1 egg

2 tablespoons almond milk

2 tablespoons coconut oil melted

2 teaspoons vanilla extract

1/3 cup walnut pieces

1/3 cup dates (chopped up a bit)

## Directions:

1. Preheat the oven to 375 degrees Fahrenheit.
2. Add the dry ingredients (almond flour, AP flour, sugar, salt, cinnamon, and baking powder) to a medium-sized bowl, and mix well.
3. Melt the coconut oil by placing it in a microwave-safe dish and microwaving it for 20-30 seconds.
4. Then add in the wet ingredients (the egg, coconut oil, almond milk, and vanilla and mix well.
5. Then add in the walnuts and dates and fold them in, so they are distributed through the batter.
6. Add spoonfuls of batter onto a silpat lined baking tray, to make 4 muffin tops, gently shaping them as necessary.
7. Bake at 375 degrees for 20-25 minutes.
8. Remove from the oven, let cool, and enjoy!

# Pistachio Double Chocolate MTs

Yield: 4 Muffin Tops

## Ingredients:

3/4 cup pistachios

1/4 cup all-purpose flour

1/3 cup sugar

1/3 teaspoon salt

1 teaspoon baking powder

1 egg

1 tablespoon almond milk

1 tablespoon coconut oil (melted)

1/2 teaspoon almond extract

1/4 cup white chocolate chips

1/4 cup semi-sweet chocolate chips

## Directions:

1. Preheat the oven to 375 degrees Fahrenheit.

2. Add the pistachios to a blender (preferably one that grinds nuts) and pulse until the pistachios are ground into a flour-like consistency. However, if you can get your hands on some store-bought pistachio flour, use that instead.

3. Add the dry ingredients (pistachio flour, all-purpose flour, sugar, salt, and baking powder) to a medium-sized bowl, and mix well.

4. Melt the coconut oil by placing it in a microwave-safe dish and microwaving it for 20-30 seconds.

5. Then add in the wet ingredients (the egg, oil, almond milk, and almond extract and mix well.

6. Fold the white chocolate chips and the semi-sweet chocolate chips into the batter so they are distributed throughout.

7. Refrigerate dough for 10 minutes so it is less runny.

8. Then add spoonfuls of batter onto a silpat lined baking tray, to make 4 muffin tops, gently shaping them as necessary.

9. Bake at 375 degrees for 20-22 minutes.

10. Remove from the oven, let cool, and enjoy!

# Spiced Oatmeal (Gluten-Free) MTs

Yield: 4 Muffin Tops

## Ingredients:

1 cup oat flour

1/3 cup brown sugar

1/3 teaspoon salt

1 teaspoon baking powder

1 teaspoon cinnamon

1/4 teaspoon cardamom

1/4 teaspoon ginger

1/2 teaspoon nutmeg

1 egg

2 tablespoons almond milk

2 tablespoon olive oil

2 teaspoons vanilla extract

## Directions:

1. Preheat the oven to 400 degrees Fahrenheit.

2. Add the dry ingredients (oat flour, brown sugar, salt, cinnamon, cardamom, ginger, nutmeg, and baking powder) to a medium-sized bowl, and mix well.

3. Then add in the wet ingredients (the egg, oil, almond milk, and vanilla and mix well.

4. Let the batter sit for 15-20 minutes in the fridge. The batter should thicken up as the oats absorb the liquid.

5. Add spoonfuls of batter onto a silpat lined baking tray, to make 4 muffin tops, gently shaping them as necessary.

6. Bake at 400 degrees for 5 minutes, then reduce heat to 350 degrees and bake at 350 degrees for 12-15

minutes. The reason for this is to get the MTs to dome well with the high heat and then not burn as they bake.

7. Remove from the oven, let cool, and enjoy!

*TIP: If you have rolled oats on hand, you can use it to make oat flour. Simply add about a cup and a half of rolled oats to a high-speed blender and blend the rolled oats on hight for about 10 seconds or until the oats are ground up into a flour-like consistency.*

# Orange Chocolate Chip MTs

Yield: 4 Muffin Tops

## Ingredients:

1/2 cup almond flour
1/2 cup all-purpose flour
1/3 cup sugar
1/3 teaspoon salt
1 teaspoon baking powder
1 egg
3 tablespoons fresh orange juice
2 tablespoon olive oil
1 teaspoon orange zest
1/3 cup chocolate chips

### DRIZZLE

1/4 cup confectioners sugar
2-3 teaspoons orange juice
1/4 teaspoon orange zest

## Directions:

1. Preheat the oven to 375 degrees Fahrenheit.
2. Add the dry ingredients (almond flour, AP flour, sugar, salt, and baking powder) to a medium-sized bowl, and mix well.
3. Then add in the wet ingredients (the egg, fresh orange juice, and oil, and mix well.
4. Fold in the orange zest and the chocolate chips so the are distributed well through the batter.
5. Add spoonfuls of batter onto a silpat lined baking tray, to make 4 muffin tops, gently shaping them as necessary.
6. Bake at 375 degrees for 20-22 minutes.
7. Remove from the oven, let cool.
8. Make the drizzle by mixing together the powdered sugar and orange juice. Drizzle over the cooled MTs, then decorate with remaining orange zest and enjoy!

# Flax Oatmeal (Gluten-Free) MTs

Yield: 4 Muffin Tops

## Ingredients:

1/2 cup ground flax
1/2 cup oat flour
1/3 cup brown sugar
1/3 teaspoon salt
1 teaspoon baking powder
1 teaspoon cinnamon
1/4 teaspoon cardamom
1/4 teaspoon ginger
1/4 teaspoon nutmeg
1 egg
2 tablespoons almond milk
2 tablespoon olive oil
1 teaspoon vanilla extract

## Directions:

1. Preheat the oven to 375 degrees Fahrenheit.
2. Add the dry ingredients (ground flax, oat flour, brown sugar, salt, cinnamon, cardamom, ginger, nutmeg, and baking powder) to a medium-sized bowl, and mix well.
3. Then add in the wet ingredients (the egg, oil, almond milk, and vanilla and mix well.
4. Add spoonfuls of batter onto a silpat lined baking tray, to make 4 muffin tops, gently shaping them as necessary.
5. Bake at 375 degrees for 18-20 minutes.
6. Remove from the oven, let cool, and enjoy with honey!

TIP: If you have rolled oats on hand, you can use it to make oat flour. Simply add about a cup and a half of rolled oats to a high-speed blender and blend the rolled oats on hight for about 10 seconds or until the oats are ground up into a flour-like consistency.

*A bite of these Lemon Muffin Tops is like a taste of summer in your mouth. These ones are so delicately soft on the inside and ever so slightly crisp on the outside, with a strong lemon flavor. And they are made without any eggs, making them vegan-friendly!*

# Iced Lemon MTs

Yield: 4 Muffin Tops

## Ingredients:

1 cup all-purpose flour

1/3 cup sugar

1/3 teaspoon salt

1 teaspoon baking powder

3 tablespoons olive oil

5 tablespoons almond milk

1 teaspoon lemon zest

2 tablespoons lemon juice

DRIZZLE

1/4 cup confectioners sugar

2-3 teaspoons fresh lemon juice

1/4 teaspoon lemon zest to garnish

## Directions:

1. Preheat the oven to 350 degrees Fahrenheit.

2. Add the dry ingredients (the flour, sugar, salt, and baking powder) to a medium-sized bowl, and mix well.

3. Then add in the wet ingredients (the oil, almond milk, lemon juice, and lemon zest, and mix well. BTW, when zesting the lemon, carefully zest off the yellow part without the white flashy part underneath.

4. Add spoonfuls of batter onto a silpat lined baking tray, to make 4 muffin tops, gently shaping them as necessary.

5. Bake at 350 degrees for 20-25 minutes.

6. Remove from the oven and let cool.

7. Make the drizzle by mixing together the confectioners sugar and lemon juice and drizzle on top of the cooled MTs. Sprinkle the lemon jest on top and enjoy!

# Red Velvet MTs *with* Cream Cheese Filling

Yield: 4 Muffin Tops

## Ingredients:

3/4 cup almond flour

1/4 cup cocoa powder

1/4 cup all-purpose flour

1/3 cup Truvia® blend

1/3 teaspoon salt

1 teaspoon baking powder

1 egg

1 tablespoon olive oil

2 tablespoons almond milk

1 teaspoon vanilla extract

2 tablespoons grated raw beetroot (approximately half of a small beetroot)

1 teaspoon white vinegar


**CREAM CHEESE FILLING**

4 tablespoons cream cheese

2 tablespoons powdered sugar


**DRIZZLE**

1/4 cup powdered sugar

2 teaspoons white vinegar

## Directions:

1. Preheat the oven to 375 degrees Fahrenheit.
2. Peel a small beetroot and grate it using a microplane grater. In this case it is important to use a microplane grater and not a vegetable grater as the microplane grater will grate the beetroot into smaller shreds than a vegetable grater would. This would help the beetroot evenly color the MTs.
3. Add the dry ingredients (almond flour, cocoa powder, AP flour, Truvia®, salt, and baking powder) to a medium-sized bowl, and mix well.
4. Then add in the wet ingredients (the egg, oil, almond milk, grated beetroot, vinegar, and vanilla and mix well.
5. Make the filling by mixing together the cream cheese and the powdered sugar well.
6. Then add a spoonful of batter onto a silpat lined baking tray, to make the base of a muffin top. Repeat this step 3 more times so there are a total of 4 bases of muffin tops.
7. Place a spoonful of the cream cheee filling on top of the bases of the MTs.
8. Divide spoonfuls of the remaining batter between the four MTs, covering up the cream cheese filling as much as possible (as seen in the picture above).
9. Bake at 375 degrees for 18-20 minutes.
10. Remove from the oven and let cool.
11. When cool, make the drizzle by mixing together the powdered sugar and vinegar. Then drizzle on top of the MT's and enjoy!

# Strawberry Chocolate Chip MTs

Yield: 4 Muffin Tops

## Ingredients:

1/2 cup almond flour

1/2 cup ground oats

1/3 cup Truvia® blend
(sugar and stevia blend)

1/3 teaspoon salt

1 teaspoon baking powder

1 egg

1 tablespoon almond milk

1 tablespoon olive oil

1 teaspoon vanilla extract

1/3 cup chocolate chips

3 large strawberries
(chopped up)

## Directions:

1. Preheat the oven to 375 degrees Fahrenheit.
2. Add the dry ingredients (almond flour, ground oats, Truvia® blend, salt, and baking powder) to a medium-sized bowl, and mix well.
3. Then add in the wet ingredients (the egg, oil, almond milk, and vanilla and mix well.
3. Chop up the strawberries into little chunks and add those to the batter.
4. Also add in the chocolate chips and fold these into the batter.
5. Add spoonfuls of batter onto a silpat lined baking tray, to make 4 muffin tops, gently shaping them as necessary.
6. Bake at 375 degrees for 20-22 minutes.
7. Remove from the oven, let cool, and enjoy!

TIP: If you have rolled oats on hand, you can use it to make oat flour. Simply add about a cup and a half of rolled oats to a high-speed blender and blend the rolled oats on hight for about 10 seconds or until the oats are ground up into a flour-like consistency.

# Sugar Free MTs

*Made with frozen blueberries, these refined sugar-free muffin tops are such a hit, whenever I make them. Sometimes, I add some lemon zest of orange zest for even more flavor!*

# Blueberry MTs

Yield: 4 Muffin Tops

## Ingredients:

1/2 cup all-purpose flour
1/2 cup almond flour
1/2 cup monk fruit sweetener
1/3 teaspoon salt
1 teaspoon baking powder
2 tablespoons olive oil
2 tablespoons unsweetened almond milk
1 egg
1 teaspoon vanilla extract
1/2 cup frozen blueberries

## Directions:

1. Preheat the oven to 375 degrees Fahrenheit.
2. Add the dry ingredients (almond flour, all-purpose flour, monk fruit sweetener, salt, and baking powder) to a medium-sized bowl, and mix well.
3. Then add in the wet ingredients (the egg, oil, almond milk, and vanilla and mix well.
4. Add in the frozen blueberries and fold these into the batter.
5. Add spoonfuls of batter onto a silpat lined baking tray, to make 4 muffin tops, gently shaping them as necessary.
6. Bake at 375 degrees for 18-20 minutes.
7. Remove from the oven, let cool, and enjoy!

# Peach Pecan MTs

Yield: 4 Muffin Tops

## Ingredients:

1/2 cup all-purpose flour

1/2 cup almond flour

1/2 cup monk fruit sweetener

1/3 teaspoon salt

1 teaspoon baking powder

2 tablespoons olive oil

2 tablespoons almond milk

1 egg

1 teaspoon vanilla extract

1 small peach (approx 1/2 cup)

1/3 cup pecan pieces

## Directions:

1. Preheat the oven to 375 degrees Fahrenheit.
2. Add the dry ingredients (almond flour, all-purpose flour, monk fruit sweetener, salt, and baking powder) to a medium-sized bowl, and mix well.
3. Then add in the wet ingredients (the egg, oil, almond milk, and vanilla and mix well.
4. Rinse off the peach, remove the seed, then chop it up and fold the peach chunks, along with the pecan pieces into the batter.
5. Chill the batter for 20 minutes in the fridge.
6. Add spoonfuls of batter onto a silpat lined baking tray, to make 4 muffin tops, gently shaping them as necessary.
7. Bake at 375 degrees for 18-20 minutes.
8. Remove from the oven, let cool, and enjoy!

# Spiced Pear MTs

Yield: 4 Muffin Tops

## Ingredients:

1/2 cup all-purpose flour

1/2 cup almond flour

1/2 cup monk fruit sweetener

1/3 teaspoon salt

1 teaspoon baking powder

1/4 + 1/4 teaspoon cinnamon

1/4 teaspoon ginger

1/4 teaspoon cardamom

1/4 teaspoon nutmeg

1/4 teaspoon cloves

1 tablespoons olive oil

2 tablespoons almond milk

1 egg

1 teaspoon vanilla extract

1/2 cup chopped pear and

4 thin slices of pear to decorate

(about 1 medium pear)

## Directions:

1. Preheat the oven to 375 degrees Fahrenheit.
2. Add the dry ingredients (almond flour, all-purpose flour, monk fruit sweetener, salt, baking powder, 1/4 teaspoon cinnamon, ginger, cardamom, nutmeg, and cloves) to a medium-sized bowl, and mix well.
3. Then add in the wet ingredients (the egg, oil, almond milk, and vanilla and mix well.
4. Rinse off the pear, then chop up half of it (or enough for 1/2 a cup) and fold the pear chunks into the batter.
5. Chill the batter for 20 minutes in the fridge.
6. Add spoonfuls of batter onto a silpat lined baking tray, to make 4 muffin tops, gently shaping them as necessary.
7. Slice the remaining pear and use slices to decorate the top of each muffin top.
8. Sprinkle each muffin top with the remaining 1/4 teaspoon of cinnamon
9. Bake at 375 degrees for 18-20 minutes.
10. Remove from the oven, let cool, and enjoy!

*The texture on these almond flour muffin tops are simply amazing. Light and airy and not too filling, yet jam packed with protein and almond flavor!*

# Almond (Gluten-Free) MTs

Yield: 4 Muffin Tops

## Ingredients:

1 cup almond flour

1/2 cup monk fruit sweetener

1/3 teaspoon salt

1 teaspoon baking powder

3 tablespoons olive oil

2 tablespoons almond milk

1 egg

1 1/2 teaspoons vanilla extract

1/2 teaspoons almond extract

## Directions:

1. Preheat the oven to 350 degrees Fahrenheit.

2. Add the dry ingredients (almond flour, monk fruit sweetener, salt, and baking powder) to a medium-sized bowl, and mix well.

3. Then add in the wet ingredients (the egg, oil, almond milk, almond extract, and vanilla extract and mix well.

4. Add spoonfuls of batter onto a silpat lined baking tray, to make 4 muffin tops, gently shaping them as necessary.

5. Bake at 350 degrees for 20 minutes.

6. Remove from the oven, let cool, and enjoy!

# Avocado Cardamom MTs

Yield: 4 Muffin Tops

## Ingredients:

1/2 cup all-purpose flour
1/2 cup almond flour
1/2 cup monk fruit sweetener
1/3 teaspoon salt
1 teaspoon baking powder
1/4 teaspoon cardamom
1 avocado mashed
1 tablespoons almond milk
1 egg
1 teaspoon vanilla extract
1/4 teaspoon almond extract

## Directions:

1. Preheat the oven to 375 degrees Fahrenheit.
2. Add the dry ingredients (almond flour, all-purpose flour, monk fruit sweetener, salt, cardamom, and baking powder) to a medium-sized bowl, and mix well.
3. Then cut open the avocado and add the fleshy part into the bowl with the dry ingredients. Using a fork, mash up the avocado.
4. Then add in the wet ingredients (the egg, almond milk, and vanilla) and mix well.
5. Add spoonfuls of batter onto a silpat lined baking tray, to make 4 muffin tops, gently shaping them as necessary.
6. Bake at 375 degrees for 20-22 minutes.
7. Remove from the oven, let cool, and enjoy!

# Peanut Chip MTs

Yield: 4 Muffin Tops

## Ingredients:

1/2 cup all-purpose flour

1/2 cup almond flour

1/3 cup monk fruit sweetener

1/3 teaspoon salt

1 teaspoon baking powder

1/2 teaspoon nutmeg

3 tablespoons olive oil

2 tablespoons almond milk

1 egg

1 teaspoon vanilla extract

1/2 cup + 1 tablspoon sugar free Reeses peanut chips

## Directions:

1. Preheat the oven to 375 degrees Fahrenheit.

2. Add the dry ingredients (almond flour, all-purpose flour, monk fruit sweetener, salt, nutmeg, and baking powder) to a medium-sized bowl, and mix well.

3. Then add in the wet ingredients (the egg, oil, almond milk, and vanilla and mix well.

4. Fold the 1/2 cup of sugar-free Reeses peanut chips into the batter.

5. Add spoonfuls of batter onto a silpat lined baking tray, to make 4 muffin tops, gently shaping them as necessary.

6. Scatter the remaining 1 tablspoon of Reeses Peanut Chips on the tops of the MTs.

7. Bake at 375 degrees for 20-22 minutes.

8. Remove from the oven, let cool, and enjoy!

# Raspberry White Chocolate MTs

Yield: 4 Muffin Tops

## Ingredients:

1/2 cup almond flour

1/2 cup all-purpose flour

1/3 cup monk fruit sweetener

1/3 teaspoon salt

1 teaspoon baking powder

1 egg

3 tablespoons olive oil

2 tablespoons almond milk

1 teaspoon vanilla extract

1/2 cup raspberries

1/3 cup Lilly's® white chocolate chips

## Directions:

1. Preheat the oven to 375 degrees Fahrenheit.

2. Add the dry ingredients (almond flour, all-purpose flour, monk fruit sweetener, salt, and baking powder) to a medium-sized bowl, and mix well.

3. Then add in the wet ingredients (the egg, oil, almond milk, and vanilla and mix well.

4. Fold in the raspberries and the Lilly's® white chocolate chips into the batter as well.

5. Add spoonfuls of batter onto a silpat lined baking tray, to make 4 muffin tops, gently shaping them as necessary.

6. Bake at 375 degrees for 20-22 minutes.

7. Remove from the oven, let cool, and enjoy!

# Hummingbird MTs

Yield: 4 Muffin Tops

## Ingredients:

1 cup all-purpose flour

1/3 cup monk fruit sweetener

1/3 teaspoon salt

1 teaspoon baking powder

1 teaspoon cinnamon

1/4 teaspoon cardamom

1/4 teaspoon cloves

1/4 teaspoon ginger

1/4 teaspoon nutmeg

1 banana (1/2 cup - mashed)

1/4 cup sugar-free pineapple tidbits canned (mashed with fork)

1/2 cup walnuts

1 egg

1 teaspoon vanilla extract

## Directions:

1. Preheat the oven to 375 degrees Fahrenheit.
2. Add the dry ingredients (all-purpose flour, monk fruit sweetener, salt, baking powder, cinnamon, cardamom, cloves, ginger, and nutmeg) to a medium-sized bowl, and mix well.
3. Peel and mash the banana and add it to the bowl with the dry ingredients.
4. Drain the pineapple tidbits, mash them and add them to the dry ingredients as well.
5. Then add in the rest of the wet ingredients (the egg and vanilla) and mix well.
6. Fold the walnuts into then batter too.
7. Add spoonfuls of batter onto a silpat lined baking tray, to make 4 muffin tops, gently shaping them as necessary.
8. Bake at 375 degrees for 20-22 minutes.
9. Remove from the oven, let cool, and enjoy!

# Coffee Chocolate Chip MTs

Yield: 4 Muffin Tops

## Ingredients:

1/2 cup almond flour

1/2 cup all-purpose flour

1/3 cup xylitol

1/3 teaspoon salt

1 teaspoon baking powder

2 teaspoons espresso powder

1 egg

2 tablespoons unsweetened almond milk

2 tablespoon olive oil

2 teaspoons vanilla extract

1/2 cup sugar-free chocolate chips

## Directions:

1. Preheat the oven to 375 degrees Fahrenheit.

2. Add the dry ingredients (almond flour, all-purpose flour, xylitol, salt, baking powder, and espresso powder) to a medium-sized bowl, and mix well.

3. Then add in the wet ingredients (the egg, oil, almond milk, and vanilla) and mix well.

4. Fold the sugar-free chocolate chips into the batter as well, reserving a few to scatter on top of each of the formed MTs.

5. Add spoonfuls of batter onto a silpat lined baking tray, to make 4 muffin tops, gently shaping them as necessary.

6. Scatter the remaining sugar-free chocolate chips on the tops of the MTs.

7. Bake at 375 degrees for 20-22 minutes.

8. Remove from the oven, let cool, and enjoy!

# Lemon Berry MTs

Yield: 4 Muffin Tops

## Ingredients:

1/2 cup almond flour
1/2 cup all-purpose flour
1/3 cup xylitol
1/3 teaspoon salt
1 teaspoon baking powder
1 egg
2 tablespoons unsweetened almond milk
2 tablespoon olive oil
1 teaspoon vanilla extract
1 teaspoon zest of lemon
1/2 cup mixed berries (raspberries, blackberries, blueberries)

## Directions:

1. Preheat the oven to 375 degrees Fahrenheit.
2. Add the dry ingredients (almond flour, all-purpose flour, xylitol, salt, and baking powder) to a medium-sized bowl, and mix well.
3. Then add in the wet ingredients (the egg, oil, almond milk, and vanilla) and mix well.
4. Rinse off the berries, pat them dry and add them to the batter along with the lemon zest. Fold the lemon zest and berries into the batter.
5. Add spoonfuls of batter onto a silpat lined baking tray, to make 4 muffin tops, gently shaping them as necessary.
6. Bake at 375 degrees for 20-22 minutes.
7. Remove from the oven, let cool, and enjoy!

# Walnut Chocolate Chip MTs

Yield: 4 Muffin Tops

## Ingredients:

1 cup oat flour

1/3 cup xylitol

1/3 teaspoon salt

1 teaspoon baking powder

1 egg

2 tablespoons almond milk

2 tablespoon olive oil

1 teaspoons vanilla extract

1/2 cup walnuts

1/3 cup sugar free chocolate chips

## Directions:

1. Preheat the oven to 400 degrees Fahrenheit.

2. Add the dry ingredients (oat flour, xylitol, salt, and baking powder) to a medium-sized bowl, and mix well.

3. Then add in the wet ingredients (the egg, oil, almond milk, and vanilla) and mix well.

4. Fold the walnuts and the sugar-free chocolate chips into the batter

5. Chill the batter for 15-20 minutes in the fridge so the oats absorb some of the liquid and the batter thickens up a bit.

6. Add spoonfuls of batter onto a silpat lined baking tray, to make 4 muffin tops, gently shaping them as necessary.

7. Bake at 400 degrees for 5 minutes, then reduce heat to 375 degrees and bake at 375 degrees for 12-15 minutes.

8. Remove from the oven, let cool, and enjoy!

TIP: If you have rolled oats on hand, you can use it to make oat flour. Simply add about a cup and a half of rolled oats to a high-speed blender and blend the rolled oats on hight for about 10 seconds or until the oats are ground up into a flour-like consistency.

# Double Chocolate MTs

Yield: 4 Muffin Tops

## Ingredients:

1/2 cup almond flour

1/2 cup all-purpose flour

1/3 cup xylitol

1/3 teaspoon salt

1 teaspoon baking powder

1 tablespoon instant coffee

3 tablespoons unsweetened cocoa powder

1 egg

3 tablespoons almond milk

2 tablespoon olive oil

1 teaspoon vanilla extract

1/3 cup sugar-free chocolate chips

## Directions:

1. Preheat the oven to 375 degrees Fahrenheit.

2. Add the dry ingredients (almond flour, all-purpose flour, xylitol, salt, instant coffee, unsweetened cocoa powder, and baking powder) to a medium-sized bowl, and mix well.

3. Then add in the wet ingredients (the egg, oil, almond milk, and vanilla) and mix well.

4. Fold the sugar-free chocolate chips into the batter too.

5. Add spoonfuls of batter onto a silpat lined baking tray, to make 4 muffin tops, gently shaping them as necessary.

6. Bake at 375 degrees for 20-22 minutes.

7. Remove from the oven, let cool, and enjoy!

# Savory MTs

# Beet Cheddar MTs

Yield: 4 Muffin Tops

## Ingredients:

1/2 cup all-purpose flour

1/2 cup almond flour

1/3 teaspoon salt

1 teaspoon baking powder

3 tablespoons grated raw beetroot

1 egg

3 tablespoon butter (melted)

1 tablespoon unsweetened almond milk

1/3 cup cheddar (cubed)

## Directions:

1. Preheat the oven to 375 degrees Fahrenheit.
2. Add the dry ingredients (almond flour, all-purpose flour, salt, and baking powder) to a medium-sized bowl, and mix well.
3. Peel a small beetroot and grate it using a microplane grater. In this case it is important to use a microplane grater and not a vegetable grater as the microplane grater will grate the beetroot into smaller shreds than a vegetable grater would. This would help the beetroot evenly color the MTs.
4. Melt the butter by placing in a microwave-safe dish and microwaving on high for 20 seconds or so.
5. Then add in the other wet ingredients (the egg, almond milk, and melted butter) and mix well.
6. Cut the cheddar into small cubes and fold these into the batter as well.
7. Add spoonfuls of batter onto a silpat lined baking tray, to make 4 muffin tops, gently shaping them as necessary.
8. Bake at 375 degrees for 18-20 minutes.
9. Remove from the oven, let cool, and enjoy!

# Chickpea Olive MTs

Yield: 4 Muffin Tops

## Ingredients:

1 cup all-purpose flour

1/3 teaspoon salt

1 teaspoon baking powder

1/2 teaspoon Za'atar

1 egg

3 tablespoon olive oil

5 tablespoon unsweetened
almond milk

1/4 cup chickpeas

1/4 cup olives (green or
black)

## Directions:

1. Preheat the oven to 375 degrees Fahrenheit.

2. Add the dry ingredients (all-purpose flour, salt, Za'atar, and baking powder) to a medium-sized bowl, and mix well.

3. Then add in the wet ingredients (the egg, oil, and almond milk), and mix well.

4. Slice the olives (unless they are already sliced.

5. Fold the chickpeas and olives into the batter.

6. Add spoonfuls of batter onto a silpat lined baking tray, to make 4 muffin tops, gently shaping them as necessary.

7. Bake at 375 degrees for 20 minutes.

8. Remove from the oven, let cool, and enjoy!

# Rosemary Gouda MTs

Yield: 4 Muffin Tops

## Ingredients:

1/2 cup all-purpose flour

1/2 cup almond flour

1/3 teaspoon salt

1 teaspoon baking powder

1 teaspoon fresh rosemary

1 egg

4 tablespoons butter (melted)

1 tablespoon unsweetened almond milk

1/2 cup Gouda

## Directions:

1. Preheat the oven to 375 degrees Fahrenheit.

2. Add the dry ingredients (almond flour, all-purpose flour, salt, and baking powder) to a medium-sized bowl, and mix well.

3. Melt the butter by placing in a microwave-safe dish and microwaving on high for 20 seconds or so.

4. Then add in the wet ingredients (the egg, melted butter, and almond milk) and mix well.

5. Chop up the rosemary and add this to the batter.

6. Cut the Gouda into pieces and fold this into the batter as well.

7. Add spoonfuls of batter onto a silpat lined baking tray, to make 4 muffin tops, gently shaping them as necessary.

8. Bake at 375 degrees for 20 minutes.

9. Remove from the oven, let cool, and enjoy!

# Sweet Potato Spinach Onion MTs

Yield: 4 Muffin Tops

## Ingredients:

**STUFFING**

1 sweet potato
1 small onion
1/2 cup frozen spinach
2 tablespoons oil
salt and pepper to taste
1 tablespoon harissa
saute 10-15 minutes

**MUFFIN TOPS**

1 cup all-purpose flour
1/3 teaspoon salt
1 teaspoon baking powder
1 egg
4 tablespoons melted butter
2 tablespoon unsweetened almond milk

3/4 cup of the stuffing

## Directions:

**STUFFING**

1. Peel and dice the onion and sweet potato into very small pieces.
2. Add the oil to a large pan and add in the onion and sweet potato, cover the pan with a lid and saute for about 5 minutes. Uncover, and stir the onion and sweet potato. Then, place the lid back on and saute another 5 minutes.
3. Uncover, add the spinach and harissa into the pan and saute for another 5 minutes, stirring often.
4. Remove the pan from the heat and let stuffing cool down.

**MUFFIN TOPS**

1. Preheat the oven to 375 degrees Fahrenheit
2. Add the dry ingredients (all-purpose flour, salt, and baking powder) to a medium-sized bowl, and mix well.
3. Melt the butter by placing in a microwave-safe dish and microwaving on high for 20 seconds or so.
4. Then add in the wet ingredients (the egg, melted butter, and almond milk), and mix well.
5. Add 3/4 cup of the cooled stuffing to the mix
6. Add spoonfuls of batter onto a silpat lined baking tray, to make 4 muffin tops, gently shaping them as necessary.
7. Bake at 375 degrees for 20 minutes.
8. Remove from the oven, let cool, and enjoy!

# Sundried Tomato Olive MTs

Yield: 4 Muffin Tops

## Ingredients:

1 cup all-purpose flour

1/3 teaspoon salt

1 teaspoon baking powder

1/2 teaspoon oregano

1 egg

3 tablespoon butter melted

1 tablespoon unsweetened almond milk

1/4 cup olives

3 tablespoons sundried tomatoes

## Directions:

1. Preheat the oven to 375 degrees Fahrenheit.

2. Add the dry ingredients (all-purpose flour, salt, oregano, and baking powder) to a medium-sized bowl, and mix well.

3. Melt the butter by placing in a microwave-safe dish and microwaving on high for 20 seconds or so.

4. Then add in the wet ingredients (the egg, melted butter, and almond milk), and mix well.

5. Slice the olives and the sundried tomatoes and fold them into the batter.

6. Add spoonfuls of batter onto a silpat lined baking tray, to make 4 muffin tops, gently shaping them as necessary.

7. Bake at 375 degrees for 20 minutes.

8. Remove from the oven, let cool, and enjoy!

# Cheddar Jalapeno MTs

Yield: 4 Muffin Tops

## Ingredients:

1/2 cup almond flour

1/2 cup all-purpose flour

1/3 teaspoon salt

1 teaspoon baking powder

1 egg

3 tablespoon olive oil

3 tablespoons
unsweetened almond milk

1/4 cup cheddar

1 jalapeno

## Directions:

1. Preheat the oven to 375 degrees Fahrenheit.
2. Add the dry ingredients (almond flour, all-purpose flour, salt, and baking powder) to a medium-sized bowl, and mix well.
3. Then add in the wet ingredients (the egg, oil, and almond milk), and mix well.
4. Rinse off the jalapeño and chop it up and add it to the batter.
5. Chop up the cheddar into small pieces and fold the cheddar and jalapeno into the batter.
6. Add spoonfuls of batter onto a silpat lined baking tray, to make 4 muffin tops, gently shaping them as necessary.
7. Bake at 375 degrees for 20-252 minutes.
8. Remove from the oven, let cool, and enjoy!

# About the Author

Shashi Charles is the content creator behind the food blog, Savory Spin. She is a self taught cook and baker who started her blog in the summer of 2013 as an online collection of recipes for her daughter.

She spent her childhood in Colombo, Sri Lanka, but left Sri Lanka with her parents and sister when a civil war broke out there. She spent her teen years in Abu Dhabi, with her family. After that, she came to Atlanta, GA to attend college, and it has been her home since then.

Growing up enjoying her mom's healthy home cooking, Shashi and her family rarely ever ate out. She was brought up on the concept that cooking at home is not only fun and therapeutic but, homemade recipes can be delightfully tasty and healthy at the same time. Not to mention, extremely budget-friendly as well. As a result, she strives to share her recipes, which are a nutritious, budget-friendly fusion of Sri Lankan and Middle Eastern Cuisine, with her readers. She is a huge fan of "a little spice is always nice" and passionately incorporates spices, that can be easily picked up at most grocery stores, into the eats and treats she shares on her blog.

Shashi's recipes have been featured in Buzzfeed, Delish, MSN, Taste of Home, Parade, Diabetes Strong, Insider, Food Fanatic, Brit & Co, Daily Burn, Pure Wow, Chowhound, Huffpost, and Hello Giggles. Her blog was recently featured on Toast's " The Best 50 Food Blogs in the US in 2024."

# Acknowledgments

The idea for this book happened a year ago. During that time, I made and remade so many of the muffin top recipes in these pages. And, I am so grateful to all who have supported me on this Muffin Top Mania adventure!

To my daughter, Geri, thank you for being my number-one supporter from day one. For enabling me to start my blog eleven years ago, for the incredibly constructive criticism, and for cheering me on through this book. To Steve, thank you for taste-testing so many muffin tops. Without you, I would not know that these muffin tops would still taste delicious after 2 hours on a flight, through TSA scanners, through road trips, and after months in the freezer. To my mom, Penny, and sister, Manju, for the support and encouragement through this book and for taste testing so many of the sugar-free versions.

And, to all those readers who visit my blog, Savory Spin. Thank you for making and sharing my recipes, and letting me know how much you enjoy dining in on them. And, if you happen to have picked up a copy of this cookbook, thank you for your support, it is so incredibly appreciated!

Love,

Shashi

www.ingramcontent.com/pod-product-compliance
Lightning Source LLC
Chambersburg PA
CBHW080845120626
46553CB00009B/2574